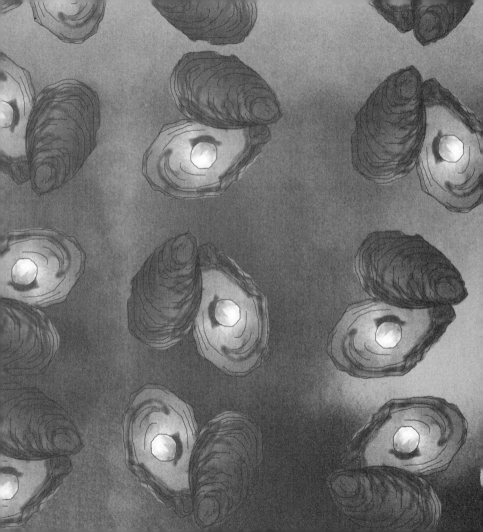

You are the
pearl in my
oyster

First Edition
20 19 18 17 16   5 4 3 2 1

Text © 2016 Gibbs Smith
Illustrations © 2016 Gibbs Smith

Published by
Gibbs Smith
P.O. Box 667
Layton, Utah 84041

1.800.835.4993 orders
www.gibbs-smith.com

Designed by Sky Hatter

Printed and bound in Hong Kong

Gibbs Smith books are printed on either recycled, 100% post-consumer waste, FSC-certified papers or on paper produced from sustainable PEFC-certified forest/controlled wood source. Learn more at www.pefc.org.

Library of Congress Cataloging-in-Publication Data
Library of Congress Control Number: 2016930181
ISBN: 9781423644774

You are the
pearl in my
oyster

Illustrated by Sky Hatter

GIBBS SMITH
TO ENRICH AND INSPIRE HUMANKIND

Wish you were here.

This song reminds me

You have my Heart.

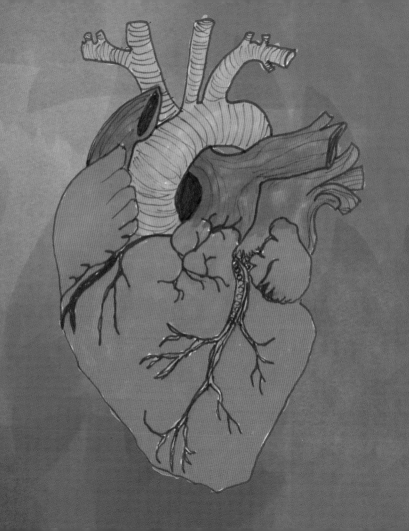

i seem to have
loved you
in numberless forms,
numberless times,
in life after life,
in age after age,

FOREVER.

—Rabindranath Tagore

If you are not too long,

I will wait here for you
ALL MY LIFE.

— *Oscar Wilde*

HOW WAS YOUR DAY?

Call me anytime,

DAY

OR

NIGHT.

I missed
you.

How can
I help?

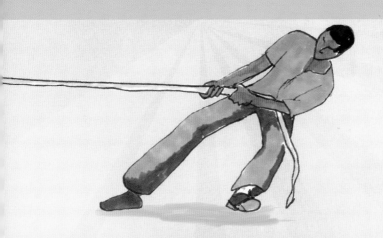

I'm
MAD
about
YOU.

You're
delicious.

YOU WERE RIGHT.

You bring out
the best in me.

You make
me smile.

You're the jam
in my jelly donut.

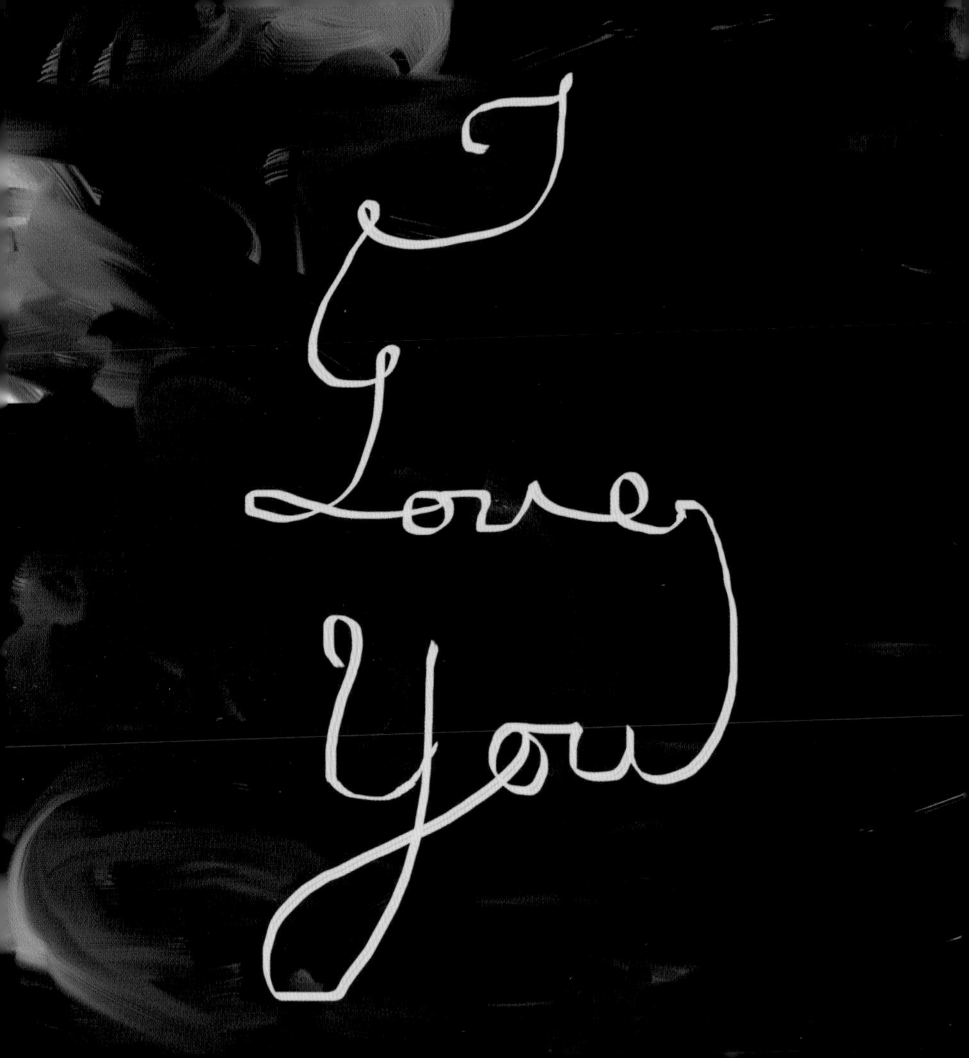
I Love You

a bushel

and a peck

and a hug
around the neck

I really,
really

really,
like you.

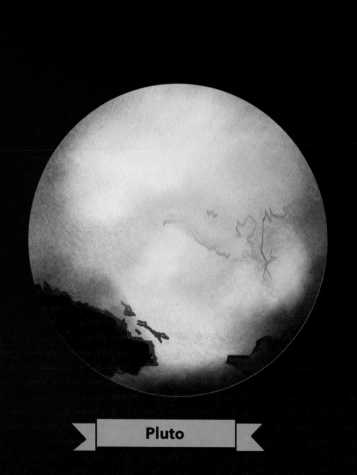

Pluto

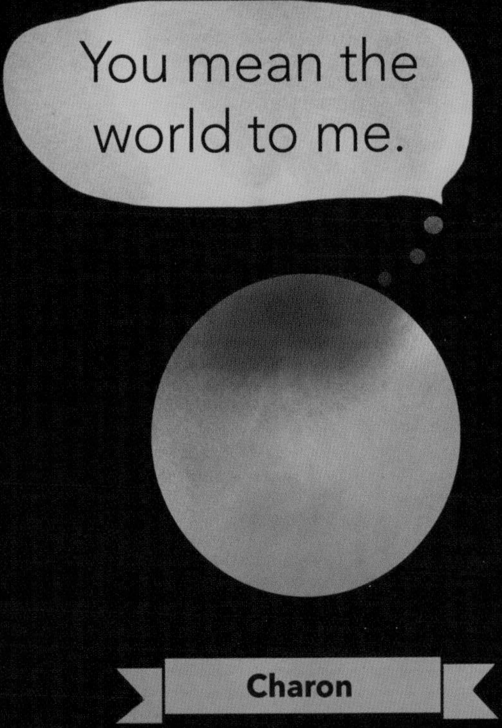
You mean the world to me.
Charon

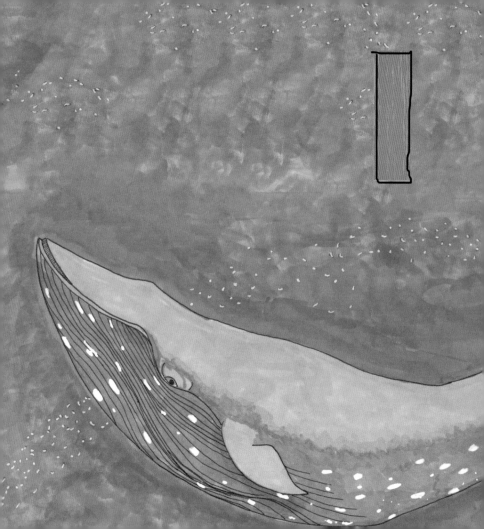

SUPER
like you.

YOU ARE
AMAZING.

take good care
of yourself

I wish I could
turn back
the clock.

I'd find you sooner
and love you longer.

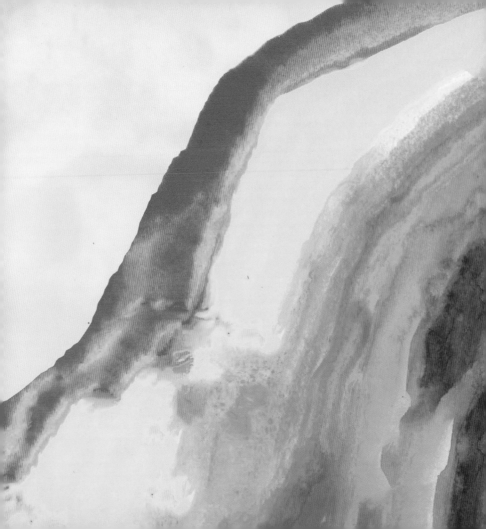

I feel so

LUCKY

to have you in

my life.

what did I

do to deserve

YOU?

You have the best laugh.

You are the cream in my coffee.

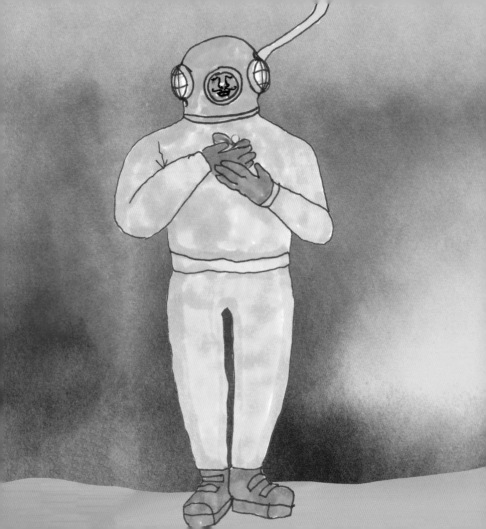

You are the

pearl in my

oyster

RAWR!

(THAT MEANS "I LOVE YOU"
IN DINOSAUR.)

You are the

best

thing that
ever happened
to me.

Fore
alw

And then my soul saw you
and it kind of went,
"Oh, there you are.
I've been looking for you."

—Iain S. Thomas

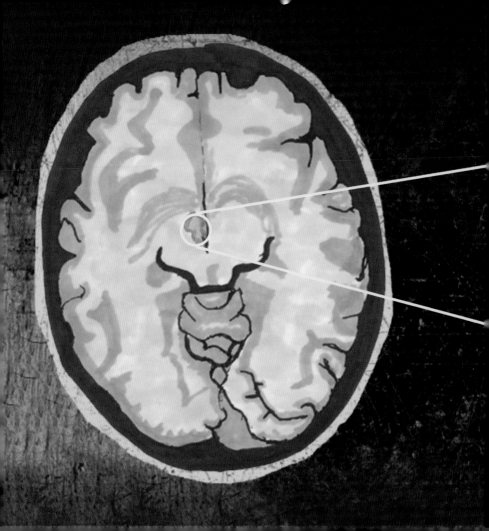

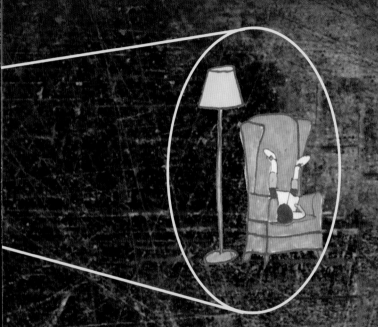

We're Just
2 lost souls
living in a
fishbowl.

—Pink Floyd

*I love you more than just
to the moon and back.*

You are every

REASON,

every

HOPE,

& every

DREAM

I've ever had.

— *Nicholas Sparks*

By night, love, tie your heart to mine, and the two together in their sleep will defeat the darkness.

—Pablo Neruda